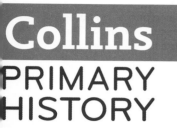

Collins
PRIMARY HISTORY

Invaders
Pupil Book

Alf Wilkinson

William Collins' dream of knowledge for all began with the publication of his first book in 1819.
A self-educated mill worker, he not only enriched millions of lives, but also founded a flourishing publishing house.
Today, staying true to this spirit, Collins books are packed with inspiration, innovation and practical expertise. They place you at the centre of a world of possibility and give you exactly what you need to explore it.

Collins. Freedom to teach.

Published by Collins
An imprint of HarperCollins*Publishers*
The News Building
1 London Bridge Street
London
SE1 9GF

Browse the complete Collins catalogue at
www.collins.co.uk

10 9 8 7 6 5 4 3 2 1

ISBN 978-0-00-831082-0

British Library Cataloguing-in-Publication Data
A catalogue record for this publication is available from the British Library.

Author: Alf Wilkinson
Publisher: Lizzie Catford
Product developer: Natasha Paul
Copyeditor: Sally Clifford
Indexer: Jouve India Private Ltd
Proofreader: Nikky Twyman
Image researcher: Alison Prior
Map designer: Gordon MacGilp
Cover designer and illustrator: Steve Evans
Internal designer: EMC Design
Typesetter: Jouve India Private Ltd
Production controller: Rachel Weaver
Printed and bound by Martins the Printers

MIX
Paper from
responsible sources
FSC™ C007454

This book is produced from independently certified FSC™ paper to ensure responsible forest management.

For more information visit:
www.harpercollins.co.uk/green

Contents

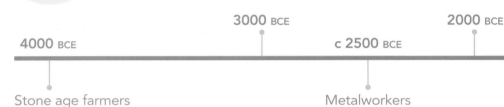

4000 BCE   3000 BCE   c 2500 BCE   2000 BCE

Stone age farmers   Metalworkers

The town of Boston, Lincolnshire

In 2016, the population of Boston, in England, was 65,000. Of these, 20 per cent were recent arrivals from the EU, mostly from Portugal, Latvia, Lithuania and Poland. The last three countries joined the **European Union** in 2004, when the **free movement of people** between countries of Europe was guaranteed. Such a rapid rate of migration has caused many changes in the town.

Map showing the location of Boston, in Lincolnshire, England

Why move to Boston?

Boston has always been an important centre for agriculture. Lincolnshire grows most of the peas, beans, salads and potatoes that England eats, and these crops are **labour-intensive**. There has been a recent growth in food processing – preparing salads and sandwiches for supermarkets, for example. In the past, people were often bussed in from nearby towns at harvest time, but now farmers often grow three crops a year, and much more labour is needed. Such work is boring, repetitive and low-paid – and most British people do not want to do it. So there has been plenty of work for migrants, usually young single people, and that has attracted people to the town.

Invaders and settlers

Over the centuries, people have always moved to Britain. Some have come as visitors, planning to stay for a while, then go home. Others have come to settle. Still others have come as invaders. Can you identify which groups on the timeline across the top of this page fit into which category?

Shops catering for recent arrivals in Boston

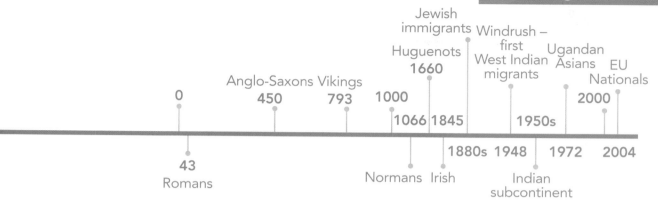

Timeline:

- 0
- 43 Romans
- Anglo-Saxons 450
- Vikings 793
- 1000
- 1066 Normans
- 1845 Irish
- Huguenots 1660
- 1880s Indian subcontinent
- Jewish immigrants
- Windrush – first West Indian migrants 1950s
- 1948
- Ugandan Asians 1972
- EU Nationals 2000
- 2004

Hengist and Horsa

It is not always easy to tell the difference between an invader or a settler. After the Romans left Britain in 410 CE, the Picts and other tribes were attacking the Britons. The King, Vortigern, invited Saxons (led by two brothers, Hengist and Horsa) from Denmark and Germany, to come and help him fight off the invaders. So initially the Saxons were invited to the country as **mercenary** troops. Once the invaders were defeated, the Saxons decided they would like to stay and sent for more troops and settlers. After defeating the Britons, the Saxons took over large parts of the south. So, were the Saxons migrants, invited to come; invaders, taking over the land; or settlers, seeking a better life than the one they left behind? Just to complicate matters, some historians regard the story of Hengist and Horsa as myth, suggesting they might not have existed, although they do agree that the Saxons were invited to the country to protect from invasion.

Think about it!

1. Make a list of all the reasons you can think of that people move home.

2. If you were moving home and could only take one small suitcase with you, what would you pack? Why?

Key words

European Union

free movement of people

labour-intensive

mercenary

oral history

Let's do it!

1. Carry out an **oral history** project. Make a list of questions you would like to ask someone from an older generation (parents, grandparents or a neighbour). Find out if they have moved, and why. Ask them what it felt like to leave and arrive, and how easy or hard it was to move.

Why the Romans came to Britain

There were already extensive trade links between Britain and the Roman Empire, and many of the rulers of tribes in the South had **treaties** with Rome. When fighting broke out between some of the tribes, Rome's good links with Britain were disrupted, and supplies of gold, tin and copper declined. There was also a new emperor in Rome, Claudius, who was keen to prove himself strong. Unlike Julius Caesar in 55 BCE and 54 BCE, he wanted to actually add Britain to the Roman Empire. With many tribes fighting each other, and some of the **deposed** rulers asking Rome for help, it seemed like a perfect opportunity to invade Britain. Claudius put together an invasion army of 40,000 men, thinking victory would be easy.

Why the Anglo-Saxons came to Britain

As we have seen in Unit 1.1, the early Anglo-Saxons were invited by the Britons to help them keep out the Picts and the Scots. Being successful, they were rewarded with land and money. Realising that Britain was wealthy, and a much better place to live than their own lands, these early Saxons sent home for more Saxons to follow them. Whole families arrived by boat, bringing with them farming tools and animals – all they needed to successfully farm the lands they occupied. It is thought that, initially, Saxons settled in the empty spaces away from the Britons. It may have taken 200 years for this to happen. It is difficult to know, however, as there are few accurate **contemporary** records. During that time some Anglo–Saxons and Britons were inter marrying, and it tended to be the more warlike Saxons that became the leaders of tribes.

Why the Vikings came to Britain

The word 'viking' means 'raider', and the first contact between Vikings and the inhabitants of Britain was in a series of raids on coastal targets. Perhaps the most famous was the attack on the monastery at Lindisfarne in 793. Successful raids brought wealth, prestige and status to individual Vikings. These first raids were usually isolated events, but then, in around 865, a 'Great Heathen Army', as the Anglo-Saxons called it, invaded and stayed over winter. Many of these Vikings were younger sons who had no land to inherit in their homeland. There is even recent research suggesting that many Vikings were looking for a bride. Gradually, Vikings turned from raiders to traders and settlers. By 1016, there was even a Viking King of England, King Cnut.

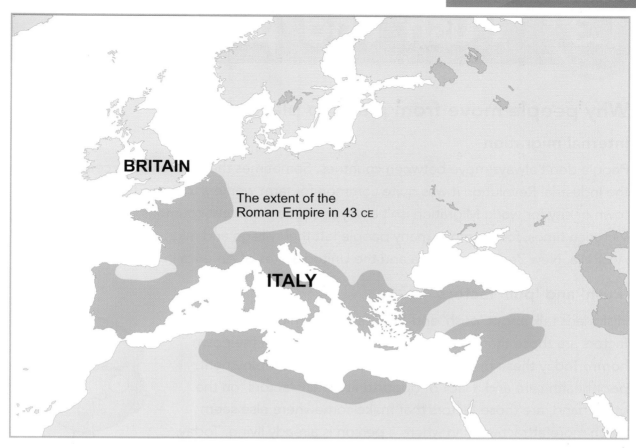

BRITAIN

The extent of the
Roman Empire in 43 CE

ITALY

The Roman Empire in c 43 CE

Think about it!

1. In what ways were the reasons for Romans, Anglo-Saxons and Vikings coming to Britain similar? In what ways were they different?
2. Can you now tell the difference between a 'raider' and an 'invader' and a 'settler'?

Let's do it!

1. Look carefully at the map. Work out where each of these groups came from.
2. Briefly research the homelands of the Romans, Anglo-Saxons and Vikings. Does that help explain why they turned their attention to Britain?
3. Which threat do you think would scare the native Britons most? Why?

Key words

treaties   deposed   contemporary

Why people move from place to place

Internal migration

People don't always move between countries. Sometimes they move within countries. In the Industrial Revolution it was quite common for farm workers to move to the nearest town or city for work. Migration isn't always between different countries, although in Victorian times, for example, many people left their village and migrated to countries like Australia, New Zealand, Canada and the United States of America in search of a better life.

'Push' and 'pull' factors

Historians talk about 'push' and 'pull' factors in migration. 'Push' factors are those that tend to drive people away from their own home. Today these might include war, poverty, unemployment, poor health care and a lack of opportunity. 'Pull' factors, on the other hand, are those factors that make somewhere else seem much more attractive than where a person is already living. Today, these might include education, good housing or a better job or **standard of living**.

People move from place to place for all kinds of different reasons.

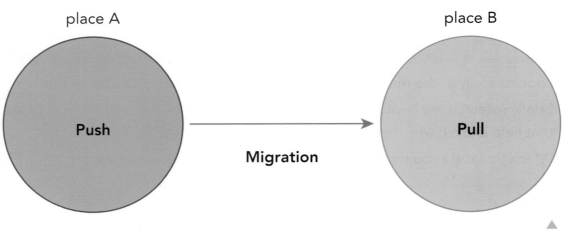

place A

place B

Push

Migration

Pull

Push and pull

Think about it!

1. Think about one very important decision you have had to make recently. How did you decide what to do?

2. Draw up a grid of the things that were 'pushing' you in one direction, and 'pulling' you in another, when you were deciding what to do.

3. Imagine you are a Roman living in Gaul, a Saxon living in Saxony, or a Viking living in Norway. A message has come to your village asking for people to come to Britain to join those already settled there. What would you do? How would you decide whether to go or to stay?

Let's do it!

1. Make a list of all the 'push' factors which influenced the Roman decision to invade Britain in 43 CE. Then make a list of the 'pull' factors. Which is longer? Which do you think was the most important factor for the Roman invasion?

2. Repeat the process for both the Anglo-Saxons and the Vikings. In each case, can you work out, from what you know already which was the most important factor? Was it 'push' or was it 'pull?'

3. Can you reach a conclusion, or do you need to know more before you can decide? We will come back to this idea later.

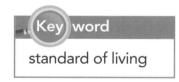

Key word

standard of living

2.1 Did the Romans ever conquer Britain?

'You're in the army now!'

Soldiers in the Roman army had to be men, at least 20 years of age, Roman **citizens**, over 1.7 metres tall, and fit. As the Empire expanded, they used conquered soldiers to fight for Rome (see page 11). They also had to be able to read and write. Soldiers signed up for 25 years, at the end of which they would receive a **pension** and some land near a Roman town where they could live and farm. Training was hard, discipline was tough, and they were expected to be able to march 30 kilometres a day in full uniform (carrying all their equipment), and build a temporary overnight camp before eating and going to bed!

Fighting

The Roman army was the strongest army the world had ever seen. Each man was taught to work together with his comrades. Most enemies were intimidated by the shield wall that was kept tight together, and it was hard to break it. Roman javelins were specially designed to prevent the enemy from throwing them back! The army also had giant catapults, called onagers, which hurled burning tar or rocks at the enemy. They also used huge wind-up crossbows called ballistas. Discipline was the key – the only times the Roman army lost battles was when the shield wall was broken or they were taken by surprise. The strength of the Roman army was the reason the Empire expanded as much as it did.

A Roman solider ▲

Roman archer, recruited from Syria or Crete. His arrows were accurate up to 400 metres ▶

Were all Roman soldiers the same?

More than half of the Roman army in Britain was made up of **auxiliaries**, who were not Roman citizens. They were recruited from the conquered parts of the Empire, such as North Africa, Germany, Gaul, Switzerland, the Middle East and Iraq. Their reward for 25 years in the army was to become a Roman citizen. Most of the cavalry was made up of auxiliaries, as were many of the archers and other specialist troops. Most were used to defend towns in forts, but they were often used in the front line of the fighting too. They were usually known after the region they were recruited in.

Roman cavalry, recruited from across the Empire, had no stirrups. The saddle was made of wood and padded, to help riders keep a better grip of the horse

Think about it!

1. If you were a Roman citizen, why might you join the army?
2. If you were not a Roman citizen, why might you join the army?
3. Why do you think the Roman army did not allow **auxiliary** units to serve in the area they came from?

Let's do it!

1. Research the Roman army – its soldiers, its weapons and its tactics. Make a presentation to the rest of your group, explaining why it was the strongest army the world had seen.
2. How important do you think auxiliaries were to the Roman army? Why?
3. Do you think all Roman soldiers were the same? Explain your answer.

When you joined the Roman army, you signed up for 25 years.

Key words

citizens

pension

auxiliaries

Invasion

In 43 CE, Emperor Claudius sent an army to invade Britain. Some leaders of the Britons accepted Roman rule, while others opposed it. One of the most famous was Caratacus, of the Catuvellauni tribe, who led the resistance. Finally defeated, he was taken to Rome as a prisoner. He is said to have made such an impressive speech before the Emperor that he was freed rather than executed, but he was not allowed to return to Britain.

It took the Romans over 30 years to conquer England and Wales. It was while the Governor Paulinus was campaigning in Wales that one of the most serious threats to Roman rule occurred.

Boudicca's revolt

In 60 CE, the leader of the East Anglian Iceni tribe died. In his will he had left half of his wealth to his wife, Boudicca, and the other half to Rome. The Romans took everything. When Boudicca objected, she was beaten. She was so angry that she led a **rebellion**, and was joined – according to some accounts – by 100,000 warriors. She led them to the Roman capital, Colchester, and burned it to the ground. You can still see the layer of ash in the soil that shows the city was destroyed. London and St Albans followed. It looked as if the Romans were going to be kicked out of Britain within 20 years of their arrival! The Roman army managed to return from North Wales just in time and stand up to the Britons. The final battle was terrible. According to Tacitus, a Roman historian writing around 100 CE, 80,000 Britons died fighting, but only 400 Romans were killed. Boudicca is said to have taken poison rather than be captured by the Romans and enslaved or killed. The last major revolt of the English was over.

You can still see the layer of ash in the soil of Colchester, where the city was burned down by Boudicca.

We don't really know all that much about Boudicca, or even what she looked like.

A Roman historian, Dio Cassius, writing around 200 CE, left this description of Boudicca:

'She was a tall woman with piercing eyes and a loud voice. A great mass of red hair hung down below her waist. Round her neck was a large gold band. She wore a long flowing tartan dress, and over it a thick cloak fastened with a brooch.'

A modern interpretation of Boudicca addressing her troops
▼

Think about it!

1. Who, in your opinion, was responsible for Boudicca's rebellion – the Iceni or the Romans?

Let's do it!

1. Which is the more useful evidence of Boudicca – the modern painting or the description of her by Dio Cassius? Why?

Key word

rebellion

Into Scotland

In 71 CE, Agricola invaded the land we now call Scotland, intending to complete the conquest of Britain. But a major victory at Mons Graupius was followed by defeats for Roman armies on the River Danube in Eastern Europe, and the troops had to be diverted to fight on the continent. A planned invasion turned into a carefully planned withdrawal. Another attempt was made in 142 CE, and the Antonine Wall was built. This was a turf wall about 60 kilometres long with a wooden **palisade** on top and a ditch to protect it, which took 12 years to complete. However, the Romans withdrew only eight years later.

The Antonine Wall took 12 years to complete and was abandoned only eight years later.

Out of Scotland?

Perhaps Scotland was not wealthy enough to attract the Romans? Perhaps the people were too warlike to defeat? Perhaps the Romans only wanted to protect the area south of Hadrian's Wall? Or maybe there were no local leaders strong enough to rule the area for them, a tactic they used successfully throughout the Empire? Whatever the reason, Hadrian's Wall became the northern border of the Roman Empire, until the Romans withdrew their forces around 410 CE.

Hadrian's Wall

In 122 CE, the Emperor Hadrian ordered a wall to be built across the country, from the River Tyne in the east to the Solway Firth in the west. The wall was 118 kilometres long, and at each mile (1.6 kilometres) there was a milecastle. Along the wall there were several forts, such as Housesteads, each of which housed 800 troops. Every fort was largely self-sufficient, with barrack rooms, granaries, baths and a hospital. The wall was 4 metres high and 3 metres thick, and protected by ditches. A road ran alongside the wall on the 'Roman' side.

The stone base of the Antonine Wall, which can still be seen today in Glasgow, Scotland

Why was Hadrian's Wall built?

Historians have several theories to explain why Hadrian ordered the building of the wall. Some say it might have been a way to keep his troops occupied in a quiet time. Others say it was to control trade between North and South – you could only cross into Roman Britain via one of the gates, and that made it easier to tax traders. The final suggestion is that it was built to keep out the Picts and Caledonians, who repeatedly attacked Roman towns, cities and farms.

The location of the Antonine Wall and Hadrian's Wall

Housesteads fort, on Hadrian's Wall, as it is today, taken from the air

Think about it!

1. Why do you think Hadrian's Wall was built?

2. Why do you think the Romans couldn't control the country we know as Scotland?

3. What does that tell us about the Caledonians and Picts, and about the Roman army?

Key word

palisade

Let's do it!

1. Research the Antonine Wall. How similar and how different was it to Hadrian's Wall? How effective a barrier would it have been?

2. Research the Battle of Mons Graupius. Where was it fought? How many were involved? How many died? What tactics did the Caledonians use? What weapons did they have? Was it a big victory for the Romans?

3. If they never conquered Scotland, can we say that the Romans conquered Britain?

Pax Romana

It wasn't all fighting and rebellion. The Roman Empire experienced a long period of peace and stability, sometimes called the Pax Romana (Roman Peace), and many Britons quickly adopted Roman ways of living. In 212 CE, all men of the Roman Empire were made citizens, giving them the same rights as Romans.

The Romans even introduced cats to Britain!

Town and countryside

Romans liked living in towns. Even so, only 10 per cent of the population lived in towns – the rest lived and worked in the countryside. Towns were small compared to today, with the biggest towns home to around 10,000 people. However, they were well planned and, like Roman forts, built on a grid system. Colchester, when it was rebuilt after Boudicca's rebellion, was surrounded by a tall, thick wall.

Houses for the rich were centrally heated, with a hypocaust underneath the floor. Towns had running water, toilets and sewers, and a bath house which was more like a modern gym. Water supply was very important and many towns were supplied by an **aqueduct**.

Rich people's houses were built around a **courtyard**, with a garden and pond in the centre. Poor people lived in simple houses, often with no form of heating and/ or cooking. Some of these houses would have a shop or craft workshop in the front room, with living space behind. Most towns had an amphitheatre where gladiators and wild animals regularly performed. Towns were the centre for government and law courts and all official business. Romans also brought Latin, the Julian calendar and numerals to Britain. Just imagine the hustle and bustle of the market in the town when traders arrived with their

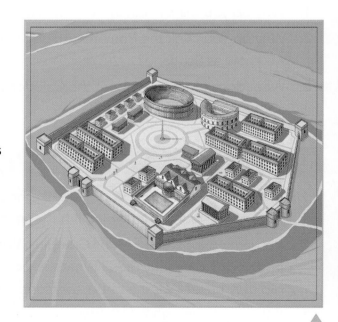

Artist's impression of a typical Roman town

goods from overseas. Towns were joined together by long, straight, well-made roads – much better than the muddy trackways of Iron Age times.

Life in the countryside

Most people still lived in Iron-Age-style **wattle and daub** houses with thatched roofs, but the rich would live in villas on their country estate. They had glass in their windows, murals on their walls, mosaics on their floors, but only small oil lamps to light each room. Villas were surrounded by gardens full of flowers, vegetables, fruit trees and medicinal herbs. There were plenty of slaves to do the work of running the household and growing the crops.

Reconstructed Roman villa, at Wroxeter, Shropshire

Copy of part of the mosaic found in Woodchester Roman villa, Gloucestershire

Think about it!

1. If you lived in Roman Britain in the 2nd century, would you have rather lived in the town or the countryside? Why?

2. What difference do you think the Romans made to most people's lives?

3. Why do you think rich Romans made mosaics of lions and tigers?

Let's do it!

1. On the artist's impression of the typical Roman town, identify: the amphitheatre, the town walls, the forum, the gates in and out of the town, the houses for the citizens.

2. Find out about Roman clothes. What did men wear? What did women wear? Were clothes the same for rich people and poor people?

3. Did Roman children go to school? If so, what did they learn?

Key words

aqueduct
courtyard
wattle and daub

Artist's impression of sea going Roman trading boat

The 'Guernsey' boat is one of only a handful of Roman sea going boats so far found outside the Mediterranean. It was about 25 metres long and made from oak planks. It caught fire and sank in the harbour in around 280 CE, and is currently being restored for display. It tells us of a strong cross-channel trade. It carried **pitch**, and pottery from both Spain and Algeria. Other imports from Europe included glass, olive oil and olives, figs and wood from the silver fir tree, which was soft and pliable and was used for wooden writing tablets like those found at Vindolanda, an important archaeological site near Hadrian's Wall. Britain exported wheat and barley to Europe, as well as lots of oysters, tin, iron and silver.

Religion

Religion was very important to Romans. Many houses had a **shrine** to their favourite god, and offerings would be left there regularly. Each town had **temples** to a wide range of gods, such as Jupiter, Neptune, Mars and Venus. New gods were added every time the Romans conquered another country – their gods were often adopted by the Romans. Sacrifices and offerings were made at temples on special days, or before taking an important decision or going on a journey.

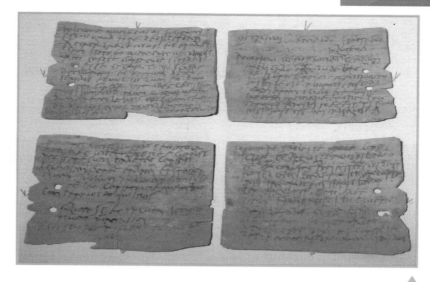

Wooden writing tablets found at Vindolanda

Think about it!

1. Does the evidence suggest that Roman Britain was a multicultural society?
2. Why do you think the Romans had so many different gods?
3. Does the fact they had so many gods explain why they were initially so opposed to Christianity?

Let's do it!

1. Find out how olives and olive oil were transported to Britain from Europe. Where exactly would these have come from?
2. Find out more about the 'Guernsey' boat. How was it built? Where might it have sailed? Are there any similar boats anywhere else? How many crew would it have needed?
3. Research the Vindolanda tablets. What do they tell us about life in Roman Britain?

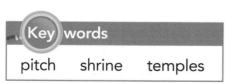

Key words

pitch   shrine   temples

The end of Roman Britain

Migration

It wasn't just goods that moved – people did too. The tomb of Barathes, a flag merchant who was born in Syria, was found in Corbridge, near Hadrian's Wall. He was 68 when he died. Nearby, in South Shields, there is the tombstone of Regina, who was first his slave and then his wife. In York we find Julia Tertia, buried with all her finery, including local **jet** jewellery as well as ivory bracelets (hence her nickname 'Ivory Bangle Lady'). She died sometime in the 4th century CE, and was possibly from North Africa, although she grew up either in the south of England or in Europe. There is increasing evidence of migration around the Roman Empire, either as traders or officials, or as wives and daughters.

Tombstone of Regina, slave and then wife of Barathes, from South Shields, Tyne and Wear Museums. She is shown in her best clothes with her jewellery box and wool for knitting

Disintegration of the Roman Empire

The Roman Empire was facing threats both from the **barbarians** (anyone who lived outside the Roman Empire) and from within (there were **civil wars** and divisions). More and more Roman troops were withdrawn from Britain to defend Rome itself. Finally, in 410 CE, the Emperor Honorius wrote to the Britons, in reply to a request for help in protecting themselves from raiders and pirates, to say that they were on their own. Rome had no troops to spare and Britain would have to look after itself from now on.

Part of a hoard of 14,865 gold, silver and bronze coins, buried in the village of Hoxne, Suffolk, UK. The owner never returned to collect them

The Dark Ages

Historians used to call the period after the Romans went home the Dark Ages. Certainly, cities and towns shrank in size and roads fell into disrepair, but many people lived as they had whilst the Romans were there. Trade carried on with Europe. People grew food and built houses, just as they always had done.

Historians used to say that civilisation came to an end as the last Roman troop left in 410 CE!

How do we know about life in Roman Britain?

Most of what we know about Roman Britain comes from the work of archaeologists, who have been investigating Roman sites for a long time. There are also some Roman remains that we can study, and lots of artefacts in museums. Tacitus, writing around 100 CE, is seen as one of the greatest Roman historians. He wrote about Agricola's campaigns in Britain. Anglo-Saxon writers such as Bede, although writing much later, tell us about the period. And, finally, place names help – 'caster' or 'chester' in a place name usually tell us it has Roman origins, for example Manchester.

Think about it!

1. In this unit you have come across lots of different types of evidence. Which do you think is the most useful in understanding Roman Britain? Why?

2. Why might historians have thought the period after the Romans left was a 'Dark Age' for Britain?

Let's do it!

1. Find out what Tacitus and Bede had to say about Roman Britain.

2. How wealthy do you think Roman Britain was?

Key words

jet
barbarians
civil wars

We have already seen how some historians thought the Romans leaving Britain plunged it into a 'Dark Age', and that Angles, Saxons, Jutes and Danes arrived in huge numbers and completely changed life for everybody forever. But is this true?

Life goes on

There is plenty of evidence that in some areas of Britain not much changed after the Romans left. One example is the Roman city of Wroxeter. It appears that, for 200 years after the Romans left, people continued to live within the city walls. The Roman buildings fell into ruins, but people lived in timber-built and thatched copies of Roman houses. Birdoswald Fort, on Hadrian's Wall, continued to be lived in, and new wooden buildings erected, long after the Romans left. Clearly, a leader had emerged and was still controlling parts of northern England!

Modern drawing showing Birdoswald Roman Fort in the 5th century – a barn on the site of a Roman granary

Everyday life

Historians think that most Anglo-Saxon settlers arrived gradually over around 200 years, and preferred to live in small villages rather than towns. They were farmers as well as fighters.

Houses were usually made from wood, with a thatched roof. A hole in the roof would let out the smoke. Doors would face east, towards the rising sun and therefore would let in the morning light. Nearby, there would be timber, fresh water and land for farming.

Farming

Anglo-Saxons kept animals such as cows, goats and sheep, as well as chickens, ducks and geese for eggs. Sometimes the animals would share the house, living at one end while the family lived in the other, especially in wintertime. Many of the animals would have to be slaughtered in the autumn and salted to preserve them – there just was not enough feed to keep all of them alive through the winter. Anglo-Saxons mostly grew einkorn (a type of wheat), rye, barley, oats, peas and beans. Vegetables like onions, leeks, turnips and cabbages were grown in gardens around the houses. Craftsmen made pottery; tools like ploughs, rakes and hoes; and clothes from leather and wool. Occasionally a trader would come to the village bringing things they could not make for themselves, or people would go to the nearest town on market day. They hunted and fished to supplement their diet whenever they could.

◄ *Ploughing, from an Anglo-Saxon manuscript*

Think about it!

1. What impact do you think the Romans leaving would have had on everyday life?
2. How similar, and how different, is the Anglo-Saxon barn to a Roman granary?

Let's do it!

1. Research Wroxeter or Birdoswald after the Romans left. Do you think this really was a 'Dark Age' for Britain?

4.2 Women

Women in Anglo-Saxon times

Women were much more equal in Anglo-Saxon times than in Roman times. No one could force them to marry if they didn't want to. A woman could leave her husband if he didn't behave in a proper way towards her. Women could own their own property – land, money, goods – and dispose of them how they saw fit. Some ran their own businesses. A woman called Eanswith, for example, was given 200 acres of land by the Bishop of Worcester in exchange for making and repairing all the special clothes (or vestments) worn by the priests in the cathedral when they were taking services.

Some jobs were mostly done by women – spinning and weaving cloth seem to have been a few of them, as were cheese-making and milking the animals. Yet it seems that many jobs were shared. Cooking, for example, wasn't always done by women – it was done by whoever had the time. At busy times of the year, women would be in the fields, like the men, sowing seed, harvesting and so on. Richer women would, as ever, supervise the household, whereas poorer women would have to work. Children would be involved in the daily household and farming tasks from an early age, learning what to do by watching and copying their parents.

Women weaving, from an Anglo-Saxon manuscript

Some women were especially important. Hilda of Whitby, for example, became very important in the church. She was abbess of the abbey at Whitby, which was made up of both monks and nuns (see Unit 5.2). Aethelflaed, the daughter of King Alfred, was educated alongside her brothers and married the King of Mercia. When he died, she ruled the kingdom in his place. She even successfully led the army in battle against the Vikings (see Unit 6.2).

A woman raising water from a well

Riddles

The Anglo-Saxons loved **riddles** and stories, and these were often told while they sat around the fire at night. Here is a popular Anglo-Saxon riddle. See if you can work out the answer:

'When I am alive I do not speak.

Anyone who wants to takes me captive and cuts off my head.

They bite my bare body

I do no harm to anyone unless they cut me first.

Then I soon make them cry.'

Think about it!

1. How easy was life for an Anglo-Saxon woman?
2. Would you prefer to be a richer or poorer woman in Anglo-Saxon times? Why?

Let's do it!

1. Find out how Anglo-Saxon women spun wool using a distaff, and wove cloth using a loom.
2. Research some Anglo-Saxon recipes and try them out. Honey, oat and spiced cakes sound particularly tasty, whereas bean cakes don't!

Key word

riddles

King Arthur

You may have heard the stories of King Arthur and his Knights of the Round Table. But the stories are just that. Geoffrey of Monmouth first wrote about Arthur in the 12th century, and Thomas Mallory added to the stories in the 15th century. But, as ever in history, there *may* have been some fact behind the stories. There probably was a Romano-British war leader, called Artorius, who led the fight against the Angles and Saxons. He may have been Welsh, or Cornish. He may have lived in Tintagel Castle, but no one is sure.

West Stow Anglo-Saxon Village

West Stow in Suffolk aims, using re-enactors and rebuilt or replica buildings, to show us what life was like in Anglo-Saxon times.

The young King Arthur pulls his sword out of the stone, confirming he is the true king. Painting by Walter Crane, 19th century

West Stow in Suffolk is a **reconstructed** Anglo-Saxon village.

West Stow Anglo-Saxon Village

Photographs of West Stow Anglo-Saxon Village

Think about it!

1. How do historians know about life in Anglo-Saxon times? Which sources would they use to find out about the past?
2. Which of these sources do you think would be most reliable?

Key word

reconstructed

Let's do it!

1. Read some of the stories about King Arthur. How realistic do you think they are?
2. Find out about 'Artorius'. Do you think he really existed?
3. Look at the photographs of West Stow Anglo-Saxon Village. Do you think the people who reconstructed this village have got it right?
4. What changes would you make to West Stow Anglo-Saxon Village? Why?
5. How useful are places like West Stow in helping us to understand life in Anglo-Saxon times?

Although most people lived and worked in the countryside, some people did live in towns, especially ports. By around 600 CE, London was beginning to grow. It developed on the north bank of the Thames, where the River Fleet met the Thames.

Hamwic

The biggest port at the time was Hamwic, which we now know as Southampton. The streets of Hamwic were laid out in a Roman-style grid pattern, with no defensive walls or fort to protect it from attack. By 700 CE, Hamwic had a population of 2000 to 3000 people. There is evidence of imports of glass from southern Spain, pottery and olive oil from Africa and quernstones from the Rhineland. Exotic spices like whole peppercorns were also imported – we know that the monk Bede kept his own private store of peppercorns to add flavour to his food! Archaeologists have also found many gold coins from Byzantium. Evidence from local shipwrecks suggests this trade was largely paid for by exporting tin ingots, although it is possible that wheat and hunting dogs, and perhaps slaves, were still exported, as in Roman times. By around 900 CE, Hamwic was in decline.

Think about it!

1. Hamwic had no defences. What does that tell us about life around 700 CE?
2. Imagine walking along the main street in Hamwic around 750 CE. What would you see? Hear? Smell? Which languages would you hear spoken?

Let's do it!

1. Compare the goods imported by Anglo-Saxons through Hamwic with those imported by the Romans. How similar are they, and how do they differ?
2. Would you still suggest that Anglo-Saxon Britain was mainly a rural country?

Why bury goods and not come back for them?

In 2009, an amazing discovery was made by two men with metal detectors in a field near Lichfield, in Staffordshire. It has been puzzling historians and archaeologists ever since. It is called the Staffordshire Hoard.

The Staffordshire Hoard

Part of the fabulous Staffordshire Hoard

So far, over 4000 items have been excavated – most are very tiny, and with one exception they were all made in England, probably during the 7th century. The one exception is a 6th-century sword **pommel** that came from Scandinavia or Germany. Each piece shows high-quality craftsmanship. The **hoard** is made up of over 5 kilograms of gold, 1.4 kilograms of silver and over 3500 pieces of garnet, a precious stone that comes from Sri Lanka or India but may also have come from Portugal or Bohemia. Every single item is associated with men – there is no women's jewellery or similar – and with soldiers. Also, most items were broken into tiny pieces. They were probably all wrapped in cloth or bags made from **flax**. It is the largest ever collection of Anglo-Saxon gold so far discovered.

Think about it!

1. Why might a rich leader bury so much wealth?
2. Why might he not come back for it?

Let's do it!

1. Research the Staffordshire Hoard. What does it tell us about the wealth of Mercia at this time?
2. What does it tell us about Britain's links with the rest of the world?
3. What does it tell us about the skill of craftworkers in Britain?

Key words

pommel
hoard
flax

Modern drawing of an Anglo-Saxon monastery, featuring a church, a kitchen, a hospital, a meeting and writing house, monks' houses, fields and vegetable gardens

Since Roman times, there had been Christians and **pagans**, often living side by side. Initially, the Anglo-Saxons brought their traditional pagan gods with them when they migrated to Britain but, over time, many became Christian.

Monasteries and abbeys

Monasteries were centres of prayer and learning. Monks and nuns prayed at least five or six times a day at special services. The rest of the time, they worked. Some grew food, some healed the sick using herbs from the garden. Many would spend their day copying out religious books, not on paper but on **vellum** made from the skin of a sheep.

Making ink

The main ingredients of black ink included gallnuts (from oak trees – the best came from Syria), gum arabic (from North Africa), vitriol (from Spain), and rainwater. It took at least two weeks to mix this all up, heat it and cool it, before it was ready to use.

Coloured inks are even more complicated!

Very few people in Anglo-Saxon England could read and write. However, the monks went to a lot of trouble to copy out their books.

Red ink used vermilion, which was made by grounding up a mineral called cinnabar. Most cinnabar came from Italy.

Green ink was made from malachite, from Spain and Israel, or from English honeysuckle, grown in the monastery garden.

Blue ink was made using indigo, from the woad plant, grown in monastery gardens. The best blue came from lapis lazuli, a mineral that at the time was quarried in one mine in Afghanistan.

Gold ink used scrapings of gold leaf cut to shape.

Silver ink used scrapings of silver leaf cut to shape.

▲ Page from the Lindisfarne Gospels, produced c715-720 by the monks of Lindisfarne Monastery, Northumbria. Each different coloured ink had to be written separately

Christian or Pagan?

Many Anglo-Saxons were buried with what archaeologists call grave goods. These showed their wealth and status in life. But some of these burials are a little confusing. The Sutton Hoo Ship Burial, for example, from around 625 CE, contains the remains of a Saxon boat, swords, helmets and shields of a leader, but also contains three bronze bowls from Byzantium, all of which have Christian symbols on them. Does that mean that the person in the grave was a Christian? Christians don't usually include grave goods when they are buried.

Think about it!

1. Do you think the Anglo-Saxons were Christians or pagans?
2. Why go to so much trouble to make ink when so few people could read and write?

Let's do it!

1. Research the life of an Anglo-Saxon monk or nun. What did they do all day? Where did they live? Were they important?
2. Make a map of the journey of all the raw materials needed to make ink. What does that tell us about the Anglo-Saxons? What does it tell us about how important religion was in Anglo-Saxon times?

Key words

pagans
vellum

31

At this time there were several different Anglo-Saxon kingdoms in the country (see map) and they frequently fought each other. A strong king would expand his territory, and a weak king would lose (even his kingdom).

Alfred... the Great?

Alfred ruled Wessex from 871 CE until his death in 899 CE. We only have one image of him from the time, from a silver penny. What kind of image is Alfred trying to show on this coin? Do you think he really looked like this?

Alfred, more than any other king, saved Wessex from the Vikings and he was the first to claim to be 'King of all the Anglo-Saxons'.

Map showing Anglo-Saxon kingdoms

Why do we call Alfred 'the Great?'

Alfred believed in justice for everyone – rich and poor, young and old – and rearranged the laws of Wessex to make sure they made sense. He was the first English king to build a navy, and built a series of defended towns, called **burghs**, so people could be safe behind walls in times of trouble. He was very religious and made many gifts to churches and monasteries. He also ordered the keeping of the *Anglo-Saxon Chronicles*, an annual record of the times. This is a valuable, if not wholly reliable, source for historians.

Silver penny showing King Alfred

King Alfred and the cakes

There is a famous story of King Alfred and the cakes. He had been defeated by the Vikings and he was hiding on a small island in the Somerset floodlands. The wife of his host was making scones, or flatbread, and had to go outside to get another bucket of water. She asked Alfred to watch the cakes. Planning how to get his country back, Alfred forgot and let the cakes burn! When she came back with the water, the woman shouted at him and beat him

with her broom. Alfred meekly accepted the beating, rather than acting powerful like a king. This story was told, many years later, to show what a wise and clever ruler Alfred was. However, it probably isn't true!

Significant individuals

Some people have a really big impact on life at the time. We say these people are significant individuals. Do you think Alfred was especially important in Anglo-Saxon times? How do you decide how important someone was at the time?

Statue of King Alfred in Wantage, where he was born. How would the sculptor know what he looked like? How has he made Alfred look ◀ 'kinglike'?

Think about it!

1. Why would people tell stories like the one about King Alfred burning the cakes? What are they meant to show?
2. Who do you think was more important in Anglo-Saxon times – powerful leaders like Alfred, or ordinary people in the villages and towns growing the crops and making goods? Why?

Let's do it!

1. In groups, find out about the different kingdoms of the Anglo-Saxons. What happened to them?
2. Research Alfred, or one of the other famous people discussed in Units 4 and 5. Make a presentation to your group on why they were significant.

Key word

burgh

The Vikings lived in Scandinavia and had developed a way of life suited to their homeland. In Norway, for instance, with its many mountains and fjords and limited amount of flat land, fishing and trading were more important than farming. They kept cows, goats, hens, geese and chickens, and grew oats, barley and rye. The summers were too short and cool to grow wheat. They grew vegetables like cabbages, onions, beans, peas and carrots in gardens around their houses, and loved eating fish – especially herring. In fact, some historians argue that one of the reasons the Vikings started to raid other countries was that they began to run out of herring! The climate was harsh – with long, cold winter nights – so houses had to be warm and cosy.

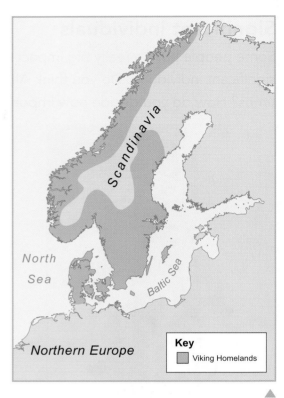

Viking Scandinavia

At home

Viking women, like most women at the time, had to obey their fathers and husbands. They were often married between the ages of 12 and 15. However, they had an unusual amount of freedom. They had complete charge of the household, including all the money. They wove cloth and made clothes, grew herbs for medicine and smoked and dried food for the winter. When men went away raiding or trading, women ran the farm too. There were slaves, or thralls, usually captured in raids or paying off debts, who did much of the hard work. A Viking lord, or Jarl, was the chief in his area and would attract warriors and supporters depending on how well he could feed and reward them. The more successful he was, the bigger his private army.

Modern photo of a reconstructed Viking longhouse

Children

Children were expected to help with jobs both inside and outside the home. They would collect berries, firewood for the winter, and would milk the animals, collect eggs, go fishing, watch the fire and help with the cooking. There was always something to do! They must also have found time to play, because archaeologists have discovered wooden swords, ships, dolls and

Modern photograph of Viking re-enactor children

animal figures, as well as spinning tops. Skating was very popular in the winter. Learning to farm and to fight were very important for boys, while girls would be taught to run the household as well as the farm, and to tend animals.

Think about it!

1. Would you say the Vikings were a rural or an urban people? Why?
2. Do you think the Viking house pictured (left) would be warm and cosy?
3. How similar, and how different, was the life of a Viking child to your own life today?

Let's do it!

1. Find out how the Vikings of Sweden and Denmark lived. Was it similar to those in Norway described here?
2. Do you think life was easier in winter or in summer?
3. In what ways were the lives of Viking women similar to those of Anglo-Saxon women?

Raid! The Viking raid on Lindisfarne

In 793 CE, a Viking raid on the monastery at Lindisfarne, Northumbria, sent shockwaves around the Anglo-Saxon world. Lindisfarne was one of the richest monasteries in the country, and a centre of learning. Ships landed and men attacked the unarmed monks, stole all the valuables and headed off back to sea before anyone could do anything about it.

More raids followed, although not all were as successful. A raid on the monastery at Jarrow in 794 CE, for example, was defeated by local Anglo-Saxon troops who had managed to get there in time because the Vikings were held up offshore by bad weather. But mostly these Viking raids were very successful, as they chose isolated, undefended targets, and took what riches and slaves they could find. Not too many slaves, however, because they wouldn't fit in the Viking longboats. Raids happened in the summer months, when the seas were calmer than in winter.

The Viking raid on Lindisfarne

The word 'Viking' means 'pirate' or 'raider'!

Early raids often were made by just two or three ships. By 830 CE, raids might involve 25–30 ships. And in 850 CE, things changed completely when a Viking army, instead of going home for the winter, set up camp on the Isle of Thanet, in Kent. They could start next year's raiding even earlier! Raiders were becoming invaders. The Anglo-Saxon kingdoms seemed more interested in fighting each other than in keeping out the Vikings.

The 'Great heathen army'

In 865 CE, not one but two Viking armies landed in England – one in Kent and the other in East Anglia. There may have been several thousand men in all. The King of East Anglia gave the Vikings horses to persuade them to go and raid elsewhere. They headed north and captured York in 866 CE and Nottingham in 867 CE. Much of the country was now in Viking hands.

Modern-day re-enactors make a shield wall

A further army arrived in 871 CE and the Vikings turned their attention to Wessex, the only kingdom still free, where King Alfred paid the Vikings to leave Wessex alone.

Why were the Vikings such good fighters?

Some Vikings wore metal armour and helmets, but most did not. They often wore thick leather padding and used shields for protection. Swords were expensive and carefully looked after, and were handed down from father to son. Most Vikings would fight with axes and spears. In battle they used a shield wall, rather like the Romans did, which was very difficult to break down. They might form a wedge to break through the enemy line, and

Viking warriors, carved from walrus ivory

of course being brave and successful in battle was the best way to become famous. Viking troops were not afraid to die fighting.

Think about it!

1. Why do you think the Viking raid on Lindisfarne was such a shock?
2. Which image of Viking warriors do you think is more useful to us – the ivory carvings or the modern-day re-enactors? Why?

Let's do it!

1. Research the 'Great Heathen Army'. Why was it so successful?
2. Find out about Viking 'berserkers'.

An artist's impression of Jorvik around 900 CE
▼

The Vikings captured York in 866 CE and it quickly became an important city. Perhaps 10,000 people lived there in the year 1000 CE. Viking York, known as Jorvik, was much bigger than any town or city anywhere in Scandinavia. People lived squashed very close together. Many would use the front room of their home as a workshop or a place to sell the goods they had produced. We know a lot about the Viking city of Jorvik because of the 'Coppergate' archaeological excavation there from 1976 to 1981. Because the ground was so damp, many things left behind by the inhabitants of Jorvik were preserved in the soil.

Viking re-enactor women spinning and weaving cloth
▼

Viking York

Houses were built very close together, out of timber and thatch, or perhaps wattle and daub. Objects discovered during the excavation tell us that the city was full of craftsmen, working in wood, bone, leather, glass, pottery and metal. Ships brought goods right into the centre of the city, up the River

Ouse, from all over the world. Silk from Constantinople; a cowrie shell from the Red Sea; quernstones from Germany; amber from the Baltic; walrus ivory from the Arctic Circle and coins from Byzantium – these were all found by archaeologists. Expensive brooches and jewellery were found, as well as thousands of everyday objects, preserved in the soil. Many dead Vikings were found in nearby churchyards, suggesting those living in the city had become Christians. Many died young, and it has been suggested that 25 per cent would die before becoming an adult, and that very few people lived to be 60.

A model of a Jorvik jeweller, at the Jorvik Viking Centre, York

There were lots of other Viking towns and cities, like Dublin in Ireland, Hedeby and Birka in Scandinavia, but the one we know most about in Britain is Jorvik.

Think about it!

1. How do the images show life in Jorvik? Where would the artists have got their information from?

2. What would it have been like to live in Viking York? How similar, and how different, would it be to living at home in Denmark?

3. What evidence is there that the Vikings traded with many countries around the world?

Let's do it!

1. Historians write about the Vikings in different ways. Some show them as skilled fighters and raiders, as at Lindisfarne or part of the 'Great Heathen Army'. Others show them as skilled craftworkers, as in Jorvik. Why do we have such different interpretations of the Vikings?

2. Is it possible that *both* views are right?

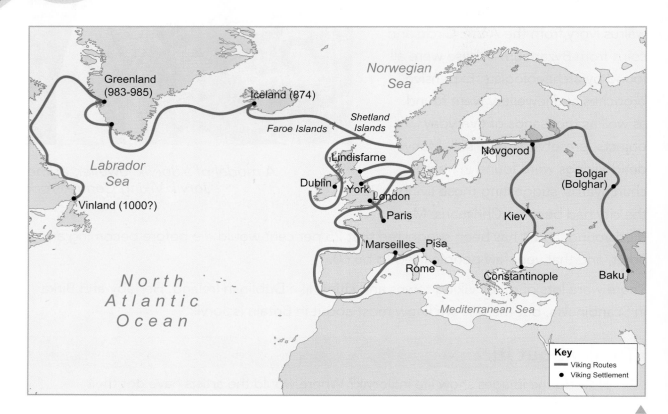

Map showing Viking routes

As you can see from the map, the Vikings sailed across much of the known world – trading, raiding and settling wherever they went.

East and south

From Sweden, Vikings went to Russia, many settling around Novgorod. Some transported their boats across land and then sailed down the River Dnepr until they reached Constantinople, the capital of Byzantium. A Viking army laid siege to the city in 860 CE, but mostly they were interested in trading for silk, silver and gold. They traded furs, walrus ivory, amber, beeswax and honey in exchange. Viking traders reached Baghdad – the biggest city in the Arab world, with a population of around 1 million – in around 850 CE. Arab leaders particularly wanted **gyrfalcons**, from Iceland and Greenland, and ivory.

The Oseberg Ship, dating from around 820 CE, found buried in a grave mound in 1904 and now on display in a museum in Oslo

West to the New World

After the raid on Lindisfarne, Vikings attacked and then settled in Ireland, around Dublin. They also settled on the Orkney, Shetland and Faroe Islands, around 800 CE, all easy journeys from Norway. By 874 CE, there were settlements on Iceland. Eric the Red is said to have discovered Greenland in 983 CE, having been blown off course on a journey from Norway to Iceland. Around 1000 CE, Leif Ericson landed in North America.

A gyrfalcon, the largest of falcons, nests along the Arctic coasts of North America, Europe and Asia

Viking ships

The secret to the success of the Vikings was the design of their ships. These came in different shapes and sizes, but the ones we are most familiar with are the longships, with dragon heads at front and rear. They could be sailed or rowed, and didn't sit low in the water, so they could sail far inland along **navigable** rivers. They had a steering oar on one side at the rear, but were designed so that they could easily change direction. There was no need to turn the boat around if they had to escape quickly from danger. There was little or no cover, so the Vikings preferred to sail in summer, when the seas were less dangerous. They also preferred to stay within sight of land if they could, which made the settlements in the Orkney, Shetland and Faroe Islands particularly important — all are just a short voyage from each other.

Key words

gyrfalcons
navigable

Think about it!

1. In what ways does this description of the Viking world change your ideas about the Vikings?
2. What would it have been like sailing from Norway to Iceland?
3. Why do you think some lands, like Greenland and Vinland, were discovered by accident?

Let's do it!

1. What do all the places visited by the Vikings have in common?
2. Find out about the Viking settlements on Iceland, Greenland and Vinland. How similar, and how different, was Viking life there to life at home in Scandinavia?
3. Research Viking ships. Were they all the same?

We have already seen (Unit 6.2) that by 871 CE only Wessex, led by King Alfred, remained as an Anglo-Saxon kingdom - the rest of the country was controlled by Vikings.

King Alfred and the Vikings

Until 878 CE, it looked very much like the Vikings would defeat Wessex, yet in 878 CE, at the Battle of Edington, Alfred decisively defeated the Vikings led by Guthrum. Guthrum agreed a truce and retreated to East Anglia, promising never to attack Wessex again. And he never did. Wessex was secure. England was split into two – a Saxon part and a Viking part known as the Danelaw.

Divided England, c 890 CE

England united

Gradually, over the next 50 years, the Anglo-Saxons, led by Aethelflaed (King Alfred's daughter), Aethelstan and Edgar, united England as one kingdom under an Anglo-Saxon ruler. Edgar, nicknamed 'The Peaceful', ruled from 957 CE to 975 CE, and in all that time there was not a single Viking raid.

War again!

Unfortunately, this did not last. Once he died Viking raids began again. In 980 CE, Hamwic (Southampton) was raided and destroyed. The Vikings attacked Thanet and Kent and won a major victory at the Battle of Maldon in 991 CE. The English decided to buy off the Vikings, paying large sums of money to them to stop the fighting. This became known as Danegeld. The Vikings began to demand more and more money in return for peace, until finally, in a desperate attempt to solve the problem, King Aethelred ordered all Vikings living in England to be killed – the so-called 'St Brice's Day Massacre'.

The St Brice's Day Massacre

Viking fury!

This only made matters worse. Svein Forkbeard, who already ruled Denmark and Norway, decided to add England to his list. By 1013 CE, he had conquered the whole country and England had a Viking king. When he died, he was followed by his son Cnut, who ruled England as well as the Scandinavian countries until he died in 1035 CE. England had a Viking king, 250 years after the Viking raid on Lindisfarne.

King Cnut the Great

Cnut brought peace to England – by paying thousands of Viking warriors to go home. To do this, he increased taxes on the Anglo-Saxons. He married Emma, who had been the wife of the previous Anglo-Saxon king, so united the Anglo-Saxon and Viking royal families. A story told about Cnut is that he made his followers carry his throne to the beach, where he ordered the sea to

Statue of King Cnut the Great in Staffordshire, England

retreat. As the tide was coming in, of course, he got wet! Henry of Huntingdon first told this story 100 years after it happened, in 1130. He says it was Cnut's way of showing he could not control everything, however many countries he ruled.

Think about it!

1. Why was it so difficult for England to unite?
2. Why did Henry of Huntingdon tell the story of Cnut and the tide?

Let's do it!

1. Make a timeline of events you have read about from the raid on Lindisfarne to the death of King Cnut. Which are the three most important events in all that time? Why?
2. Find out about life in the Danelaw. How similar was it to life in Wessex?
3. Both the kings featured here – Alfred and Cnut – are known as 'the Great'. Do they deserve the title?

Place names can give us a clue to the origins of a settlement. Here are some typical Viking names that you should easily be able to find on a map, but there are many more.

- *Beck* = stream
- *Dale* = valley
- *How* = hill
- *Kirk* = church
- *Toft* = homestead
- *Ton* = hedge or fence

▲ Cup that contained most of the buried Yorkshire Hoard

Burials often contain big clues. The Ardnamurchan ship burial, discovered in 2011, tells us about the Viking warrior buried in the ship. It dates from the 10th century and is the first complete Viking ship burial found in Britain.

Hoards. The Yorkshire Hoard was found in 2007. It had been buried in 927 CE, inside a silver cup, probably stolen from a French church. There were coins and objects from Afghanistan, Russia, Central Asia, North Africa, Europe and Ireland.

Vikings left behind many artefacts, but virtually no writing!

Museums and archaeology help us to reconstruct life at the time. Often it is the everyday items that tell us most about Viking times.

What the Anglo-Saxons said about them. The *Anglo-Saxon Chronicles* have lots to say about the Vikings and, as you would expect, not much of it is very complimentary! Why might the Anglo-Saxons not say nice things about the Vikings?

7.4 Organising an enquiry and reaching a conclusion – 'Were all Vikings the same?'

How might you answer this 'big' question about the Vikings?
What steps do you need to take?

First step: Finding the information

You will need to do some research specific to this question.

Second step: Organising your information so it helps you answer the question

You will have lots of information about the Vikings. Which will help you answer this specific question, and which can you put to one side? How do you know which information to trust? For example, is the Anglo-Saxon chronicle about the raid on Lindisfarne likely to be both accurate and true?

Think about it!

1. Do you think all Vikings were the same?
2. Do things change between 793 CE and 1066 CE?

Third step: Reaching a conclusion

You should now be able to decide your answer to the question. Remember: the conclusion you reach will depend on which evidence you trust and use.

Fourth step: Deciding the best way to present your conclusion

Do you want to write your conclusion, or make a poster or PowerPoint-type presentation? Perhaps a radio interview or a debate would work best? You must decide.

Let's do it!

1. Make a list of all the different kinds of evidence about the Vikings you have come across.
2. Sort these types of evidence by their usefulness for this enquiry.
3. Discard those that do not help *this* time.

Fifth step: Presenting your conclusion

The hard work is now over. Now all you have to do is pull it all together, making quite sure that you are answering the question and supporting your answer with evidence.

How different was life in Britain in 1066 compared to life in Roman times?

The last Viking...

Harald Hardrada was King of Norway from 1046 to 1066. In 1066, he joined Tostig, Harold Godwinson's brother, to invade England and claim the throne. After initial success, he was killed at the Battle of Stamford Bridge, near York, in September 1066. This was the last time a Viking attempted to become King of England.

The first Roman...

Julius Caesar was a powerful Roman general. He invaded Britain in both 55 BCE and 54 BCE. In 55 BCE, he made little progress, because his cavalry had been forced to return to France by a storm. In 54 BCE, he came with 5 legions and 2000 auxiliary cavalry in 800 ships, and landed near Deal. He easily defeated the Britons near Canterbury and advanced, reaching the Thames, before problems in Gaul forced Caesar to return there in September. He was probably also a little afraid of the winter seas. Caesar claimed to have conquered Britain, but was unable to actually do so.

Stained-glass window in Lerwick Town Hall showing Harald Hardrada. The Town Hall was built between 1882 and 1884

Bust of Julius Caesar, in Warsaw Park, Poland

What changed?

The Romans brought towns to Britain. But, even in Roman Britain, 90 per cent of the population lived and worked in the countryside, farming. Which crops did they grow? Were they similar to those grown by Anglo-Saxons and Vikings, or different? We know that rich Romans lived in villas, but what kind of houses did ordinary people live in? Again, how did these change between Roman times and Viking times? What did people eat? Or drink? What clothes did they wear? What did they make their clothes from? What tools did they use in their daily life, and what weapons did they use when they were fighting? How did they get about, from place to place? The Romans built long, straight roads joining up the main cities and army bases, but were there no roads in Britain before the Romans arrived. And what about after they left in 410 CE? Which gods did they believe in and pray to?

Think about it!

1. Which image is likely to be more realistic: the stained-glass window of Harald Hardrada or the statue of Julius Caesar? Why?
2. Why do you think neither of them managed to conquer Britain?

Let's do it!

1. Draw up a table like the one below. We're sure you can think of many more categories to add to the column on the left.

Category	Similar	Different
Houses		
Clothes		
Farming		
Fighting		
Living in towns and cities		
Religion		

2. Decide if you think these things were similar in Roman, Anglo-Saxon and Viking times, or different. Place a tick in the appropriate box.
3. You should now be in a position to answer the question posed at the top of this page. Just how much change has there been between 43 CE and 1066?
4. Did things change most in Roman, Anglo-Saxon or Viking times?

We have spent a lot of time in this book looking at rich and powerful leaders, often fighting each other to be in control of a kingdom or to rule England. But what about all the other people who came to Britain at this time to live a better life?

Romano-British

Rich Britons copied the Romans after they arrived, by living in villas and wearing Roman togas, learning Latin, and eating and drinking Roman food and drink. However, apart from soldiers and administrators, not that many Romans came to live in Britain, so their impact on most ordinary people was mostly limited to having to pay **taxes** and sell food and other items to the Romans.

An Anglo-Saxon carving, made from walrus ivory, traded from Vikings

Anglo-Saxons

Most Anglo-Saxons lived in small villages and hamlets, growing food and making much of what they needed themselves. They came to Britain because the land was better than their homeland. They wanted nothing more than to live peacefully and safely.

Perhaps, for most people, when there was no fighting, not that much changed...

Evidence of Saxons and Vikings living together

An 11th-century Anglo-Saxon brooch, found in Somerset. It contains Viking-style animals as part of the design

St Gregory's Church, Kirkdale, dates from Anglo-Saxon times. The South Porch contains a **sundial**, which would originally have been outside and acted as the parish clock. Beside it, there is a stone with the following inscription:

> 'Orm, the son of Gamal, bought St Gregory's church when it was broken and fallen, and had it made anew from the ground in honour of Christ and St Gregory, in the days of Edward the King and Tosti the Earl.'

Tosti, or Tostig, was Earl of Northumbria between 1055 and 1065, so the sundial dates from that time. 'Edward the King' refers to Edward the Confessor, who died in 1066. He was succeeded by Harold Godwinson, which led to the invasion by William and the Battle of Hastings. The original church was obviously much older than that and may have dated from 750 CE. Orm, who bought

The sundial at St Gregory's Church

the ruined church and rebuilt it, was the son of Gamal, and both are Scandinavian names. Gamal married the daughter of the Earl of Northumberland, so these are important people. Gamal owned lots of land in the area. The church also contains some 9th-century gravestones and the remains of Saxon or Viking stone crosses that have since been built into the church walls.

Think about it!

1. What do the carving and the brooch tell us about how Anglo-Saxons and Vikings got on together?
2. Do you think ordinary Anglo-Saxons and Vikings got on together better than powerful ones?
3. Which do you think had the most powerful impact on life in Britain – invaders or settlers?
4. Do you think Orm would have bought a ruined church in 850 CE, for example, and rebuilt it?

Let's do it!

1. Hold a class debate about 'Continuity and change in Britain from 43 CE to 1066 CE'. Which do you think was more important – change or continuity?

Key words

taxes
sundial

100 BCE	55 BCE	0	43	c 450
	Roman invasion		Roman invasion	Anglo-Saxons

A sense of period

One of the hardest skills as a historian is to develop a sense of period – what was it *really like* to live in Roman, Anglo-Saxon or Viking times?

To get to the bottom of this, you need to ask many questions, such as: Was it all fighting? Did everyone die young? Would you have had to share your house with your cows in the wintertime? Where did you go to the toilet? How did you wash your clothes? Did you even have a spare set of clothes to change into? Were conditions in the 7th century the same – or better, or worse – than in the 8th century? Was life better for rich people or for poor people? Was everyone the same in Roman Britain? We're sure you can add many more questions.

Working through this book will have helped you become something of an expert in these times, and to get some idea of the answers to these and similar questions.

92	1066	1660	1845	1880

kings   Harald Hardrada's
failed invasion

Think about it!

1. If you had a time machine, which period would you choose to visit? Would you have preferred to live in Roman Britain, Anglo-Saxon Britain, or Viking Britain? Why?

Let's do it!

1. Make a list of the advantages of living in Roman Britain, and the disadvantages. Do the same for Anglo-Saxon times and Viking times.

2. Working in small groups, see if you can agree about the 'best' time to have lived.

3. Finally, write a short article with the heading 'Why I would have preferred to live in the _____ times.'

Skills grid

Unit	Skills
1	chronology, causation
2	diversity, evidence skills
3	using evidence to reach a conclusion
4	similarity and difference
5	significance
6	interpretations
7	organising an enquiry and presenting a conclusion
8	chronology, continuity and change

9.1 History and science and technology – warfare through the ages

Why not continue the study of weapons and warfare beyond the Romans and the Vikings?

Science and technology have played a huge part in making warfare more deadly through the ages.

Romans and Vikings

We have already studied the Roman army in Unit 2. Their main weapons were sword and shield, but they also used javelins, large catapults and cavalry. Anglo-Saxons and Vikings used horses to travel to battle, but fought on foot, using swords, axes, spears and shields. How did this change post 1066?

The Normans and after

The Normans wore more armour than the Vikings, and also fought on horseback. Medieval England was the high point of the longbow, as used against the French at Crécy (1415). During the English Civil War (1642–1649) muskets and cannons became more widely used. Gunpowder had been invented by the Chinese around 700 CE, but it took a while to reach the West. By Victorian times, armies were equipped with repeater rifles, artillery and machine guns. In the First World War (1914–1918) aircraft, tanks and gas were introduced. By the Second World War (1939–1945), aircraft were far more efficient and many towns and cities were bombed, ending

Late Medieval warfare
▼

with atomic bombs being dropped on Hiroshima and Nagasaki in 1945 and historians talking about 'total war'. For the first time, everyone – soldiers and civilians – was involved in wars. During the Cold War (1947–1991), we saw the development of inter-continental ballistic missiles and the idea of mutually assured destruction ('If you attack me and kill most of my people, I will attack you at the same time and you will lose most of your people'). Warfare had become very deadly indeed! Of course, we could also include submarines, battleships and aircraft carriers at sea, as well as helicopters and jet fighters in the air.

First World War tank

An American inter-continental ballistic missile, 1970s

Think about it!

1. Why has war become more dangerous?
2. How is 'total war' different to war in Roman and Viking times?
3. We have chosen these three images to show changes in warfare through the ages. Which three pictures would you use, and why?

Let's do it!

1. Draw a timeline, from 3000 BCE to 2000 CE, and mark on it all the changes in warfare mentioned on these pages.
2. Research warfare through the ages. Add any other developments you discover to your timeline.
3. Which changes do you think were most important? Why?
4. Describe the part you think science and/or technology have played in changes in warfare through time.

9.2 History and English: Comprehension – drawing inferences

In history, it is important to be able to draw **inferences** from what you read. This means looking at the facts and coming up with a reasonable conclusion. We could describe this as 'squeezing' evidence out of all the information we can discover.

The Orkneyinga Saga

The Orkneyinga Saga, tells us about Sweyn Asleifsson (1115–1171), who was:

Viking Orkney

> '... a Viking farmer. Winter he would spend at home on Gairsay where he entertained some 80 men at his own expense... in the spring he had...a great deal of seed to sow, which he saw to carefully himself. Then when that job was done, he would go off **plundering** in the Hebrides and in Ireland on what he called his "spring-trip", then back home just after midsummer, where he stayed till the cornfields had been reaped and the grain was safely in. After that he went off raiding again till the first month of winter was ended. This he used to call his "autumn-trip".'

Using evidence

When historians look at evidence, we can make use of that evidence in different ways. We might be *quite sure* of something stated in that piece of evidence – a fact, a place, a date, an event – especially if we have other evidence that says the same thing. There are some things we might be able to deduce from evidence that is probably true, because in other circumstances the same thing has happened. For example, Sweyn *probably* grew rye for bread and oats for his animals, although the saga just talks about 'cornfields', because we know from elsewhere that Vikings grew rye, barley and oats at

Viking sagas were poems and stories telling the deeds of important and rich people, written down in Iceland in the 13th century.

this time. There are other things we might guess at. Winter evenings would be very **boisterous**, because there were 80 men sitting around with nothing to do until it was time to go off raiding in the spring.

Think about it!

1. The saga was written in Iceland, not the Orkney Islands. Does that make it more reliable, or less reliable? Why?

2. Read the extract from the Orkneyinga Saga. What can we *definitely tell* about Sweyn Asleifsson from the saga? What evidence is used to support this?

3. What can we *probably tell* about Sweyn from the saga? For example, why might he entertain about 80 men over winter? When would he need these 80 men? What would he do with them?

4. What else would we like to know about Sweyn that the extract from the saga does not mention?

Let's do it!

Drawing inferences from the evidence:

1. What kind of farmer do you think Sweyn was? How can you tell?

2. What kind of warrior do you think Sweyn was? How can you tell?

3. What kind of host do you think Sweyn was in the wintertime? How can you tell?

4. Why do you think Sweyn went raiding in the spring and autumn, when he was already rich and had lots of farmland? What does that tell us about Sweyn as a person?

5. The saga states quite clearly (line one) that Sweyn was 'a Viking farmer'. Do you think he was a farmer or a raider?

Key words

inferences

plundering

boisterous

We have studied two great **empires** in this book - the Roman Empire, and King Cnut's Scandinavian empire.

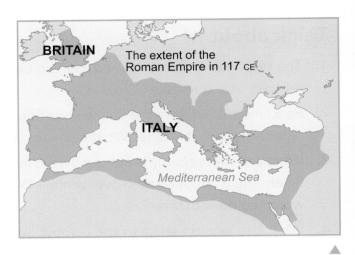

BRITAIN

The extent of the Roman Empire in 117 CE

ITALY

Mediterranean Sea

The Roman Empire

The Roman Empire

Empires are created when one country conquers and takes over other countries. The Roman Empire covered most of the Mediterranean region. This meant that goods and wealth from those countries were used to pay for the Roman army, and to make the city of Rome very, very, rich.

Empires therefore made the imperial power – in this case, Rome – richer, and the conquered country, or **colony** – in this example, Britain – poorer. They also caused a lot of fighting and wars between places, as countries tried to escape from Roman power, and become **independent**. That is what finally happened to the Roman Empire in the 5th century, when barbarians (which is what Rome called anyone who lived outside their empire) attacked and destroyed the city of Rome and the empire split into pieces.

Colonies – the example of British India

Some historians argue that being a colony *might* bring benefits to a country. For example, India was part of the British Empire for many years. The British built railways in India, introduced Western-style education and other things that might be seen as making life better. Nevertheless, other historians argue that the British were *very bad* for India, because they took lots of money from India to make Britain rich. Before India became part of the British Empire, its textile industry was the biggest in the world. The British replaced this with cotton from its factories in the Industrial Revolution, thus making many Indians poorer. Also, the British

Christmas in India, from a British magazine, December 1881

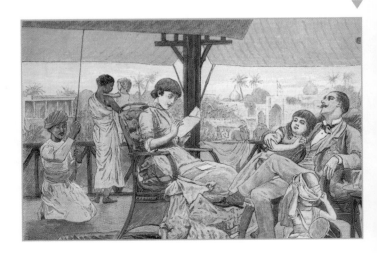

replaced Indians as rulers of that country, and ruled in a way that suited Britain, not India.

Many other countries throughout history have had their own empires: Ancient Sumer; Baghdad around 800 CE; the Mongols under Genghis Khan; the Russian Empire; the Chinese Empire under the Qing Dynasty; the Ottomans; the Spanish, French and German empires, and many more. At one time, people thought that a country could only be rich and powerful if it had its own big empire.

The British Empire in 1921

The end of empires

Since the Second World War, most countries of the world that were colonies have become independent countries, running their own affairs and acting the way they think best. In fact, there are now nearly 200 different countries in the world, whereas in 1900 there were only 55.

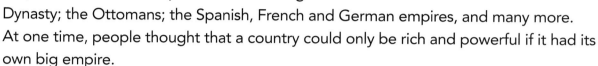

Think about it!

1. What are the advantages of having an empire? What are the disadvantages?
2. What are the advantages of being a colony? What are the disadvantages?
3. Why do you think countries wanted to be independent?

Let's do it!

1. Research the history of one empire that you find particularly interesting. What do you need to know about that empire? Make a list of key questions, and then try to discover the answers.

2. Compare the empire you have researched with empires others in your class have investigated. How similar, and how different, are they?

3. In your view, are empires a good or a bad thing? Why?

Key words

empires
colony
independent

Glossary

Aqueduct: a bridge to carry water from one place to another

Auxiliaries: 'helper' troops that were not Romans

Barbarians: according to the Romans, anyone who was NOT a Roman citizen

Boisterous: noisy fun

Burgh: town with a wall around it to protect it from invaders

Citizens: people belonging to a country, being born there

Civil wars: wars between people living in the same country

Colony: country controlled by another country; part of an empire

Contemporary: dating from the time

Courtyard: open space surrounded by buildings

Deposed: removed from ruling

Empires: lots of countries ruled by one country for its own benefit

European Union: Countries of Europe that joined together to make them stronger in the world

Flax: plant grown to make cloth

Free movement of people: no limit on people moving between the countries of the European Union

Gyrfalcons: falcons that are especially good for hunting

Hoard: collection of treasure that has been buried

Independent: country running their own affairs; not controlled by another country

Inferences: conclusions based on the evidence studied

Jet: black material used for making jewellery

Labour-intensive: need lots of workers

Mercenary: soldiers from another country paid to defend in this case England

Navigable: rivers you can sail along

Oral history: interviewing and talking to people to find out about the past

Pagans: non-Christians

Palisade: wooden fence

Pension: wage to live on after you finish working

Pitch: a kind of tar used to waterproof ships or wooden barrels

Plundering: stealing other people's goods

Pommel: ornamental top part of a sword handle

Rebellion: fight against the rulers of a country

Reconstructed: built to look like something from the past

Riddles: stories designed to be puzzles

Shrine: special place to worship a god

Standard of living: how much people earn, the way people live their lives

Sundial: clock that uses the sun to tell the time

Taxes: payment made to governments and rulers

Temples: buildings for worship

Treaties: special agreements

Vellum: kind of paper made from the skin of a sheep

Wattle and daub: building material – walls made from wooden strips covered in clay, straw and animal dung

Index

North Pole

GREENLAND

ICELAND

NORWA

UNITED
KINGDOM DENMA

IRELAND

GERMA

AU

FRANCE

CF

PORTUGAL   SPAIN

IT

CANADA

MOROCCO

ALGERIA

UNITED STATES
OF AMERICA

MAURITANIA   MALI

NIGE

MEXICO

CUBA

SENEGAL

JAMAICA

GUINEA

NIGERI

GUATEMALA

NICARAGUA

VENEZUELA

GHANA

COSTA RICA

GUYANA

PANAMA

COLOMBIA

ATLANTIC
OCEAN

Equator

ECUADOR

GABON

PERU

BRAZIL

PACIFIC
OCEAN

BOLIVIA

PARAGUAY

CHILE

URUGUAY

ARGENTINA

SOUTHERN (

South Pole

ARCTIC OCEAN

RUSSIA

NE

KAZAKHSTAN

MONGOLIA

JAPAN

PACIFIC
OCEAN

JRKEY

TURKMENISTAN

SYRIA

AFGHANISTAN

CHINA

AEL

IRAQ

IRAN

JORDAN

PAKISTAN

NEPAL

PT

SAUDI
ARABIA

OMAN

INDIA

MYANMAR

DAN

ERITREA YEMEN

THAILAND

PHILIPPINES

VIETNAM

UTH
DAN

ETHIOPIA

SRI
LANKA

SOMALIA

MALAYSIA

KENYA

Equator

TANZANIA

INDIAN
OCEAN

INDONESIA

PAPUA NEW
GUINEA

MOZAMBIQUE

SOLOMON
ISLANDS

MADAGASCAR

VANUATU

AUSTRALIA

NEW
ZEALAND

Acknowledgements

The publishers wish to thank the following for permission to reproduce images. Every effort has been made to trace copyright holders and to obtain their permission for the use of copyright materials. The publishers will gladly receive any information enabling them to rectify any error or omission at the first opportunity.

(t = top, c = centre, b = bottom, r = right, l = left)

p4b John Morrison/Alamy Stock Photo; p10t Ivy Close Images/Alamy Stock Photo; p10b DEA PICTURE LIBRARY/Contributor/Getty Images; p11 DEA PICTURE LIBRARY/Contributor/Getty Images; p14 Kay Ringwood/Alamy Stock Photo; p15b robertharding/Alamy Stock Photo; p17t Richard Allen/Alamy Stock Photo; p17b The Picture Art Collection/Alamy Stock Photo; p18 Lanmas/Alamy Stock Photo; p19 The Print Collector/Alamy Stock Photo; p20t Tombstone of Regina (stone), Roman, (2nd century CE)/Arbeia Roman Fort & Museum, Tyne & Wear Archives & Museums/© Tyne & Wear Archives & Museums/Bridgeman Images; p20b Print Collector/Contributor/Getty Images; p22 Heritage Image Partnership Ltd/Alamy Stock Photo; p23 Classic Image/Alamy Stock Photo; p24 Timewatch Images/Alamy Stock Photo; p25 De Luan/Alamy Stock Photo; p26t Lebrecht Music & Arts/Alamy Stock Photo; p27l Archimage/Alamy Stock Photo; p26b Joana Kruse/Alamy Stock Photo; p27r Andrew Palmer/Alamy Stock Photo; p29 Marco Secchi/Alamy Stock Photo; p31 Heritage Image Partnership Ltd/Alamy Stock Photo; p32b Heritage Image Partnership Ltd/Alamy Stock Photo; p33 Greg Balfour Evans/Alamy Stock Photo; p34b Danita Delimont/Alamy Stock Photo; p35 Gonzales Photo/Alamy Stock Photo; p36 Niday Picture Library/Alamy Stock Photo; p37t Richard Peel/Alamy Stock Photo; p37b Photo 12/Contributor/Getty Images; p38b Rob Watkins/Alamy Stock Photo; p39 VisitBritain/Britain on View/Getty Images; p40b Rob Watkins/Alamy Stock Photo; p41 Rosemarie Kappler/Shutterstock; p42b De Luan/Alamy Stock Photo; p43 Stephen Dorey/Alamy Stock Photo; p44 World History Archive/Alamy Stock Photo; p46t LatitudeStock/Alamy Stock Photo; p46b seawhisper/Shutterstock; p48t Heritage Image Partnership Ltd/Alamy Stock Photo; p48b © The Trustees of the British Museum. All rights reserved.; p49 Alan Curtis/Alamy Stock Photo; p50l Heritage Image Partnership Ltd/Alamy Stock Photo; p50r Joana Kruse/Alamy Stock Photo; p52 Chronicle/Alamy Stock Photo; p53t Chronicle/Alamy Stock Photo; p53b US Air Force Photo/Alamy Stock Photo; p56b Chronicle/Alamy Stock Photo.